LAUREL COUNTY PUBLIC LIBRARY

Healthy Eating with MyPyramid

The Milk Group

by Mari C. Schuh

Consulting Editor: Gail Saunders-Smith, PhD

Consultant: Barbara J. Rolls, PhD
Guthrie Chair in Nutrition
The Pennsylvania State University
University Park, Pennsylvania

Capstone
press

Mankato, Minnesota

Pebble Plus is published by Capstone Press,
151 Good Counsel Drive, P.O. Box 669, Mankato, Minnesota 56002.
www.capstonepress.com

Copyright © 2006 by Capstone Press. All rights reserved.
No part of this publication may be reproduced in whole or in part, or stored in a retrieval system, or transmitted in any form or by any means, electronic, mechanical, photocopying, recording, or otherwise, without written permission of the publisher. For information regarding permission, write to Capstone Press, 151 Good Counsel Drive, P.O. Box 669, Dept. R, Mankato, Minnesota 56002.
Printed in the United States of America

1 2 3 4 5 6 11 10 09 08 07 06

Library of Congress Cataloging-in-Publication Data
Schuh, Mari C., 1975–
    The milk group / by Mari C. Schuh.
    p. cm.—(Healthy eating with MyPyramid)
    Summary: "Simple text and photographs present the milk group, the foods in this group, and examples of healthy eating choices"—Provided by publisher.
    Includes bibliographical references and index.
    ISBN-13: 978-0-7368-5373-6 (hardcover)
    ISBN-10: 0-7368-5373-1 (hardcover)
    1. Dairy products—Juvenile literature. 2. Nutrition—Juvenile literature. I. Title.
TX377.S38 2006
641.3'7—dc22   2005023699

Credits
Jennifer Bergstrom, designer; Kelly Garvin, photo researcher; Stacy Foster and Michelle Biedscheid, photo shoot coordinators

Photo Credits
Capstone Press/Karon Dubke, cover, 3, 5, 6–7, 9, 11, 12–13, 15, 16–17, 19, 21, 22 (all)
Getty Images Inc./Seymour Hewitt, 1
U.S. Department of Agriculture, 8, 9 (inset)

The author dedicates this book to Joseph Quam of Byron, Minnesota.

Capstone Press thanks Hilltop Hy-Vee employees in Mankato, Minnesota, for their helpful assistance with photo shoots.

Information in this book supports the U.S. Department of Agriculture's MyPyramid for Kids food guidance system found at http://www.MyPyramid.gov/kids. Food amounts listed in this book are based on an 1,800-calorie food plan.

The U.S. Department of Agriculture (USDA) does not endorse any products, services, or organizations.

Note to Parents and Teachers

The Healthy Eating with MyPyramid set supports national science standards related to nutrition and physical health. This book describes and illustrates the milk group. The images support early readers in understanding the text. The repetition of words and phrases helps early readers learn new words. This book also introduces early readers to subject-specific vocabulary words, which are defined in the Glossary section. Early readers may need assistance to read some words and to use the Table of Contents, Glossary, Read More, Internet Sites, and Index sections of the book.

Table of Contents

The Milk Group

Milk, cheese, yogurt.

How many dairy products

have you had today?

Foods in the milk group
have calcium.
Your bones and teeth
need calcium to grow
healthy and strong.

MyPyramid for Kids

MyPyramid teaches you how much to eat from each food group. The milk group is part of MyPyramid.

MyPyramid For Kids

Eat Right. Exercise. Have Fun.

To learn more about healthy eating, go to this web site: www.MyPyramid.gov/kids Ask an adult for help.

Kids should eat
and drink 3 cups
from the milk group
every day.

Enjoying the Milk Group

Wow! Look at all the kinds of milk. Choose low-fat milk and low-fat dairy foods.

White, pink, brown.

If you don´t like white milk,

try chocolate or strawberry.

Which one is your favorite?

Sweet, smooth, and creamy.

Dip fruit in your yogurt

for a tasty treat.

Hard, soft,

yellow, or white.

Find many kinds

of low-fat cheese

at your grocery store.

The milk group is
a part of a healthy meal.
What are your favorite foods
made from milk?

How Much to Eat

Most kids need to have 3 cups from the milk group every day. To get 3 cups, pick three of your favorite milk products below.

Pick three of your favorite milk products to enjoy today!

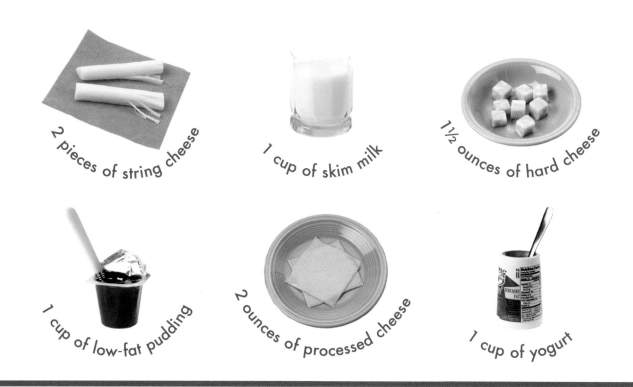

2 pieces of string cheese

1 cup of skim milk

1½ ounces of hard cheese

1 cup of low-fat pudding

2 ounces of processed cheese

1 cup of yogurt

1 cup + 1 cup + 1 cup = 3 cups

Glossary

calcium—a mineral that the body uses to build teeth and bones

dairy—foods that are made with milk; milk, cheese, and yogurt are kinds of dairy foods.

MyPyramid—a food plan that helps kids make healthy food choices and reminds kids to be active; MyPyramid was made by the U.S. Department of Agriculture.

Read More

Klingel, Cynthia Fitterer, and Robert B. Noyed. *Milk and Cheese.* Let's Read About Food. Milwaukee: Weekly Reader Early Learning Library, 2002.

Nelson, Robin. *Dairy.* First Step Nonfiction. Minneapolis: Lerner, 2003.

Rondeau, Amanda. *Milk Is Magnificent.* What Should I Eat? Edina, Minn.: Abdo, 2003.

Index

Word Count: 142
Grade: 1
Early-Intervention Level: 14

Internet Sites

FactHound offers a safe, fun way to find Internet sites related to this book. All of the sites on FactHound have been researched by our staff.

Here's how:

1. Visit *www.facthound.com*

2. Type in this special code **0736853731** for age-appropriate sites. Or enter a search word related to this book for a more general search.

3. Click on the **Fetch It** button.

FactHound will fetch the best sites for you!